# BLUES GUITAR RIFFS

T0045002

ISBN-13: 978-0-634-03222-6
ISBN-10: 0-634-03222-4

**HAL•LEONARD®**
CORPORATION
7777 W. BLUEMOUND RD. P.O. BOX 13819 MILWAUKEE, WI 53213

Visit Hal Leonard Online at
**www.halleonard.com**

# CONTENTS

# All Your Love (I Miss Loving)

Words and Music by Otis Rush

**Intro**
**Moderate Blues** ♩ = 128

\* Chords symbols reflect overall harmony.

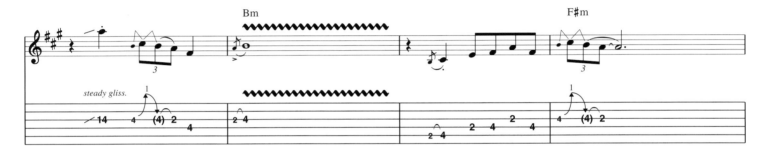

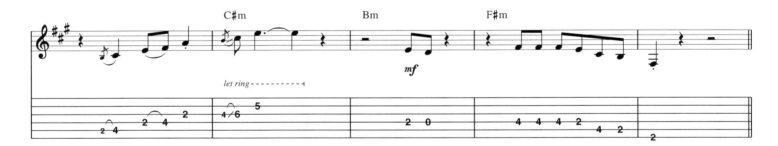

**Artist:** Otis Rush
**Album:** *This One's a Good Un*
**Year:** 1957 (single), 1968 (album)
**Guitarist:** Otis Rush

**Trivia:** Rush is a left-handed guitarist who plays a right-handed guitar upside down but not restrung. As a result, the bends he played in this riff were pulled down instead of pushed up.

# Boogie Chillen No. 2

**Words and Music by John Lee Hooker and Bernard Besman**

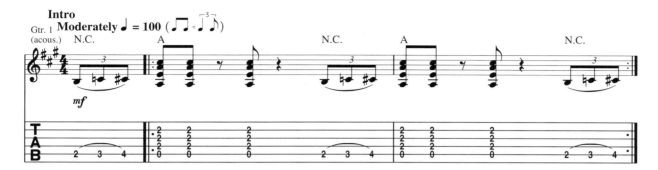

| | |
|---|---|
| **Artist:** John Lee Hooker<br>**Album:** *Burning Hell*<br>**Year:** 1948 (single), 1959 (album)<br>**Guitarist:** John Lee Hooker | **Trivia:** This song appears on not only the Rock and Roll Hall of Fame's list of 500 Songs That Shaped Rock and Roll, but also the Songs of the Century list organized by the Recording Industry Association of America, National Endowment for the Arts, and Scholastic Inc. |

# Boom Boom

**Words and Music by John Lee Hooker**

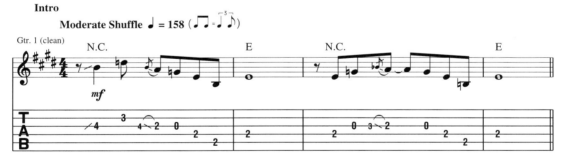

| | |
|---|---|
| **Artist:** John Lee Hooker<br>**Album:** *Burnin'*<br>**Year:** 1962<br>**Guitarists:** John Lee Hooker, Larry Veeder | **Trivia:** James Jamerson, Benny Benjamin and Hank Cosby of the legendary Motown session group the Funk Brothers played on Hooker's recording of this track. |

# Born Under a Bad Sign

Words and Music by Booker T. Jones and William Bell

Track 4

**Artist:** Albert King
**Album:** *Born Under a Bad Sign*
**Year:** 1967
**Guitarists:** Albert King, Steve Cropper

**Trivia:** Among the many covers of this blues standard is one sung by Homer Simpson on 1990's *The Simpsons Sing the Blues* album, which features B.B. King playing guitar.

# Cross Road Blues
## (Crossroads)

Words and Music by Robert Johnson

Track 6

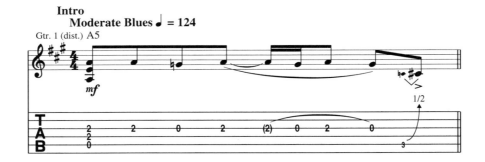

**Artist:** Cream
**Album:** *Wheels of Fire*
**Year:** 1968
**Guitarist:** Eric Clapton

**Trivia:** This song is not only a cover of the Robert Johnson classic, but it also borrows some lyrics from another Johnson song called "Traveling Riverside Blues."

# Cold Shot

**Words and Music by Mike Kindred and Wesley Clark**

Tune down 1/2 step:
(low to high) Eb–Ab–Db–Gb–Bb–Eb

\* T = Thumb on 6th string
\*\* Chord symbols reflect overall harmony.

| | |
|---|---|
| **Artist:** Stevie Ray Vaughan and Double Trouble<br>**Album:** *Couldn't Stand the Weather*<br>**Year:** 1984<br>**Guitarists:** Stevie Ray Vaughan, Jimmie Vaughan | **Trivia:** The woman who plays Stevie's love interest in this song's music video is Margaret Wiley, an actress, writer, choreographer and costume/prop designer who was voted Funniest Person in Austin, Texas in 1988. |

# Damn Right, I've Got the Blues

**By Buddy Guy**

**Artist:** Buddy Guy
**Album:** *Damn Right I've Got the Blues*
**Year:** 1991
**Guitarists:** Buddy Guy, Neil Hubbard

**Trivia:** *Damn Right, I've Got the Blues* broke a long studio album hiatus for Guy in 1991. It was obviously well worth the wait, as it won a GRAMMY® award that year for Best Contemporary Blues Album.

# 55th Street Boogie

**By Hound Dog Taylor**

Track 8

**Artist:** Hound Dog Taylor

**Album:** *Hound Dog Taylor and the HouseRockers*

**Year:** 1971

**Guitarists:** Hound Dog Taylor, Brewer Phillips

**Trivia:** Hound Dog was a polydactyl (he had a small sixth finger on each hand) who played inexpensive Japanese guitars through Sears Roebuck amplifiers with cracked speakers.

# Good Morning Little Schoolgirl

**Words and Music by Sonny Boy Williamson**

Track 9

**Artist:** Jonny Lang

**Album:** *Lie to Me*

**Year:** 1997

**Guitarists:** Jonny Lang, Billy Franzee, Ted Larsen (baritone)

**Trivia:** The recognition Jonny gained after the release of *Lie to Me* earned him cameos in the film *Blues Brothers 2000* and an episode of *The Drew Carey Show* in 1998.

# Got to Hurry

**By Oscar Rasputin**

| | |
|---|---|
| **Artist:** The Yardbirds<br>**Album:** *For Your Love*<br>**Year:** 1965<br>**Guitarists:** Eric Clapton, Chris Dreja | **Trivia:** Eric Clapton was not credited in the *For Your Love* liner notes for playing guitar on this and other songs from the album. |

---

# I Believe I'll Dust My Broom

**Words and Music by Robert Johnson**

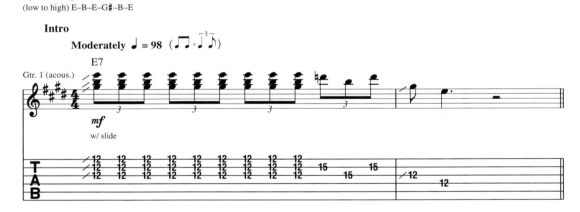

| | |
|---|---|
| **Artist:** Robert Johnson<br>**Album:** *The Complete Recordings*<br>**Year:** 1936<br>**Guitarist:** Robert Johnson | **Trivia:** *The Complete Recordings* box set was the first collection of Blues recordings to sell 1 million units. |

# I Ain't Got You

**By Calvin Carter**

| | |
|---|---|
| **Artist:** The Yardbirds<br>**Album:** *For Your Love*<br>**Year:** 1965<br>**Guitarists:** Eric Clapton, Chris Dreja | **Trivia:** This B-side of the Yardbirds rendition of "Good Morning Little Schoolgirl" is a cover of a song by bluesman Jimmy Reed. It is another song on the *For Your Love* album to which Eric Clapton was not credited in the liner notes. |

# I'm Your Hoochie Coochie Man

**Written by Willie Dixon**

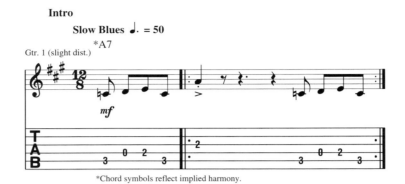

*Chord symbols reflect implied harmony.

**Artist:** Muddy Waters

**Album:** *Muddy Waters*

**Year:** 1954

**Guitarists:** Muddy Waters, Jimmy Rogers

**Trivia:** This song was written by Willie Dixon, who also played bass on the track.

---

# Let Me Love You Baby

**Words and Music by Willie Dixon**

**Artist:** Buddy Guy

**Album:** *I Was Walking Through the Woods*

**Year:** 1974 (compilation of songs from his early-1960s Chess Records era)

**Guitarists:** Buddy Guy, Lacy Gibson

**Trivia:** This was one of the songs Chess Records would occasionally allow Guy to record under his own name when he worked for the label as a session guitarist, but it was not released as a single.

# Killing Floor

**Words and Music by Chester Burnett**

Intro
Moderate Blues ♩ = 120

*Chord symbols reflect overall harmony.

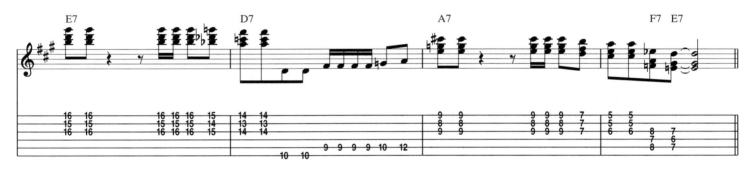

| | |
|---|---|
| **Artist:** Howlin' Wolf<br>**Album:** *The Real Folk Blues*<br>**Year:** 1966<br>**Guitarist:** Hubert Sumlin | **Trivia:** This song was essentially covered by Led Zeppelin as "The Lemon Song" but Howlin' Wolf was not credited on the *Led Zeppelin II* album. Chess Records sued for plagiarism after Wolf's death. |

# Mannish Boy

Words and Music by McKinley Morganfield (Muddy Waters), M.R. London and Ellas McDaniel

*Chord symbols reflect overall harmony.

| | |
|---|---|
| **Artist:** Muddy Waters<br>**Album:** *The Real Folk Blues*<br>**Year:** 1955 (single), 1965 (album)<br>**Guitarists:** Muddy Waters, Jimmy Rogers | **Trivia:** A variation of this riff was used in an earlier Waters song "I'm Your Hoochie Coochie Man," as well as the George Thorogood hit "Bad to the Bone." The song is also similar to "I'm a Man" by Bo Diddley. |

# Rollin' Stone (Catfish Blues)

Written by McKinley Morganfield (Muddy Waters)

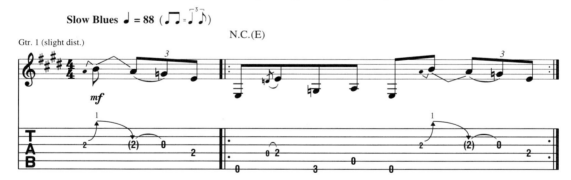

| | |
|---|---|
| **Artist:** Muddy Waters<br>**Album:** *Best of Muddy Waters*<br>**Year:** 1950 (single), 1958 (album)<br>**Guitarist:** Muddy Waters | **Trivia:** "Rollin' Stone (Catfish Blues)" was the second song to be released as a single by Chess Records. |

# Mary Had a Little Lamb

**Written by Buddy Guy**

*Chord symbols reflect basic harmony.

**Artist:** Buddy Guy

**Album:** *A Man and the Blues*

**Year:** 1968

**Guitarists:** Buddy Guy, Wayne Bennett

**Trivia:** Buddy Guy's daughter is rapper Shawnna, who was featured on Ludacris's #1 hit "Stand Up."

# Pride and Joy

**Written by Stevie Ray Vaughan**

Tune down 1/2 step:
(low to high) Eb–Ab–Db–Gb–Bb–Eb

**Intro**
**Moderate Shuffle** ♩ = 122

* Chord symbols represent overall harmony.

<table>
<tr><td>Artist: Stevie Ray Vaughan and Double Trouble</td><td>Trivia: The monumental Texas Flood album spent more than six months on the U.S. charts, which was very unusual for a blues recording in the 1980s.</td></tr>
<tr><td>Album: Texas Flood</td><td></td></tr>
<tr><td>Year: 1983</td><td></td></tr>
<tr><td>Guitarist: Stevie Ray Vaughan</td><td></td></tr>
</table>

# Rock Me Baby

**Words and Music by B.B. King and Joe Bihari**

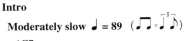

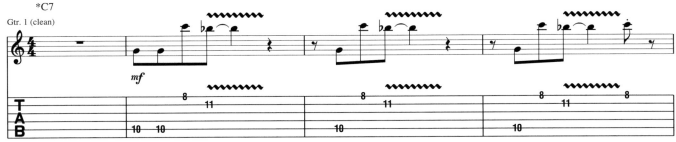

*Chord symbols reflect basic harmony.

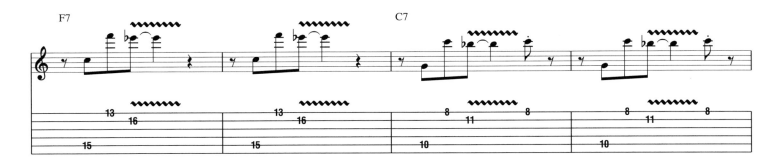

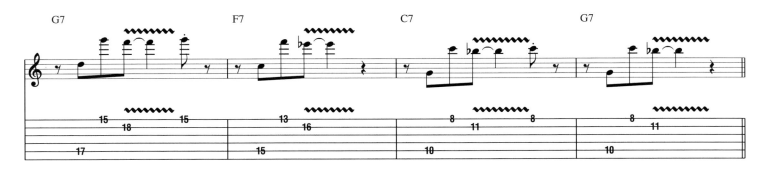

**Artist:** B.B. King
**Album:** *Rock Me Baby*
**Year:** 1964
**Guitarist:** B.B. King

**Trivia:** RPM/Kent Records had retained much of King's unreleased masters after he left the label in 1961, and released them even though he had moved on to ABC-Paramount Records. This song was the most successful of those singles, hitting the Top 40 at #34.

# Rocket 88

**Words and Music by Jackie Brenston**

Tune down 1/2 step:
(low to high) Eb–Ab–Db–Gb–Bb–Eb

**Intro**
**Moderately fast** ♩ = 150

\* Chord symbols reflect basic harmony.

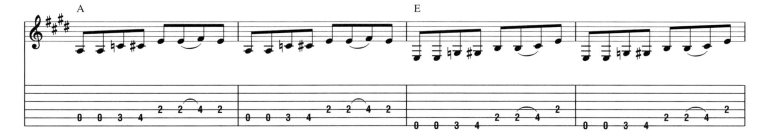

**Artist:** Jackie Brenston & His Delta Cats

**Album:** none (only released as a single by Jackie Brenston)

**Year:** 1951

**Guitarist:** Willie Kizart

**Trivia:** Bill Haley and the Saddlemen (an early name for Bill Haley & His Comets) recorded a country and western version of this song only a few months after Jackie Brenston & His Delta Cats recorded their version. However, Brenston's version is the one considered to be the first Rock & Roll record by the Rock 'n' Roll Hall of Fame.

# Satisfy Susie

**Words and Music by Lonnie McIntosh and Tim Drummond**

† Tune down 1 step, Capo III:
(low to high) D–G–C–F–A–D

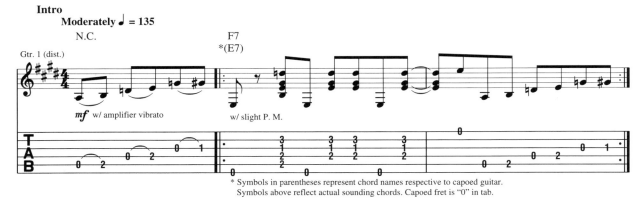

\* Symbols in parentheses represent chord names respective to capoed guitar.
Symbols above reflect actual sounding chords. Capoed fret is "0" in tab.

† Editor's note: You can accomplish the same result without tuning down a whole step by remaining in standard tuning and capoing at the first fret.

| **Artist:** Lonnie Mack<br>**Album:** *Strike Like Lightning*<br>**Year:** 1985<br>**Guitarists:** Lonnie Mack,<br>Stevie Ray Vaughan | **Trivia:** Lonnie Mack's *Strike Like Lightning* album was co-produced by Mack and Stevie Ray Vaughan, who has named Mack as an influence. |
|---|---|

# Smokestack Lightning

**Words and Music by Chester Burnett**

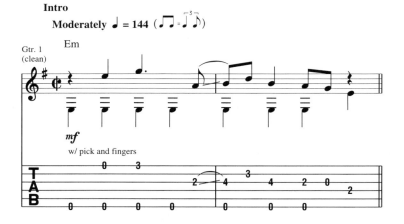

| **Artist:** Howlin' Wolf<br>**Album:** *Moanin' in the Moonlight*<br>**Year:** 1956 (single), 1962 (album)<br>**Guitarist:** Hubert Sumlin | **Trivia:** This song was covered by the Yardbirds in 1964, the Animals in 1966, and both Soundgarden and George Thorogood in 1988. |
|---|---|

# Sweet Home Chicago
### Words and Music by Robert Johnson

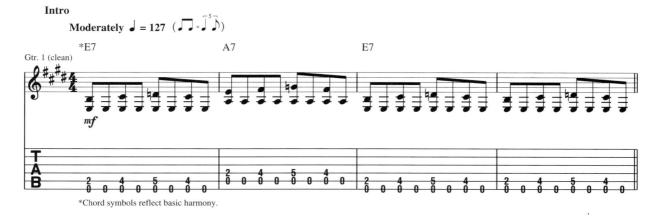

*Chord symbols reflect basic harmony.

**Artist:** Robert Johnson
**Album:** *The Complete Recordings*
**Year:** 1936
**Guitarist:** Robert Johnson

**Trivia:** A line that appears in many cover versions of this song, "Back to the same old place," was sung "Back to the land of California" by Johnson.

# Tuff Enuff
### Words and Music by Kim Wilson

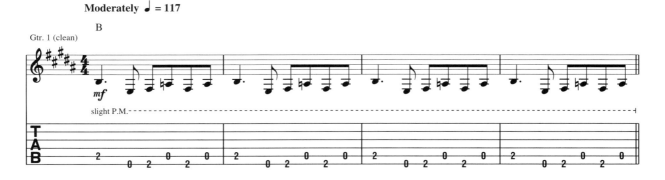

**Artist:** The Fabulous Thunderbirds
**Album:** *Tuff Enuff*
**Year:** 1986
**Guitarist:** Jimmie Vaughan

**Trivia:** This song, along with "Wrap It Up," the other single from the *Tuff Enuff* album, were featured in the 1986 film *Tough Guys.*

# Wall of Denial

**Written by Stevie Ray Vaughan and Doyle Bramhall**

**Track 26**

Tune down 1/2 step:
(low to high) Eb–Ab–Db–Gb–Bb–Eb

**Artist:** Stevie Ray Vaughan and Double Trouble
**Album:** *In Step*
**Year:** 1989
**Guitarist:** Stevie Ray Vaughan

**Trivia:** *In Step*, the last Stevie Ray Vaughan and Double Trouble studio album released while Vaughan was alive, won the GRAMMY award in 1989 for Best Contemporary Blues Album.

# Wang Dang Doodle

**Written by Willie Dixon**

**Track 27**

Drop D tuning:
(low to high) D–A–D–G–B–E

**Artist:** Koko Taylor
**Album:** *Koko Taylor*
**Year:** 1966
**Guitarists:** Buddy Guy, Johnny Twist

**Trivia:** Not only was this Koko Taylor's signature song, it was also the last single released on Chess Records to hit the R&B Top Ten, where it peaked at #4.

# Wham

**By Lonnie McIntosh**

† Tune down 1 step, Capo III:
(low to high) D–G–C–F–A–D

**Fast Blues/Rock** ♩ = 196

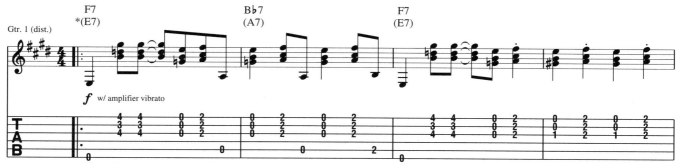

\* Symbols in parentheses represent chord names respective to capoed guitar.
Symbols above reflect actual sounding chords. Capoed fret is "0" in tab.
Chord symbols reflect basic harmony.

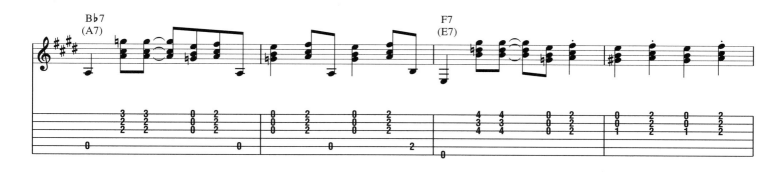

† Editors note: You can accomplish the same result without tuning down a whole step by remaining in standard tuning and capoing at the first fret.

**Artist:** Lonnie Mack
**Album:** *The Wham of That Memphis Man*
**Year:** 1964
**Guitarist:** Lonnie Mack

**Trivia:** Lonnie Mack played bass as well as a guitar solo for "Roadhouse Blues" from The Doors' *Morrison Hotel* album in 1970. He also played bass on the song "Maggie Magill" from the same album.

# Who Do You Love

### Words and Music by Ellas McDaniel

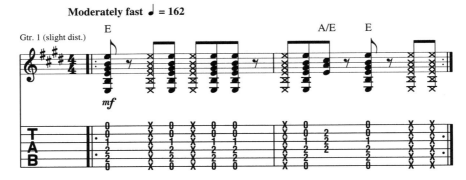

| **Artist:** Bo Diddley | **Trivia:** Though Bo Diddley's version of this song was never |
|---|---|
| **Album:** *Bo Diddley* | a hit single, it managed to make waves in the rock world, |
| **Year:** 1957 | prompting covers by such artists as Quicksilver Messenger |
| **Guitarist:** Bo Diddley | Service, The Band, Juicy Lucy, The Doors, Brownsville Station, George Thorogood and Carlos Santana. |

# You Shook Me

### Written by Willie Dixon and J.B. Lenoir

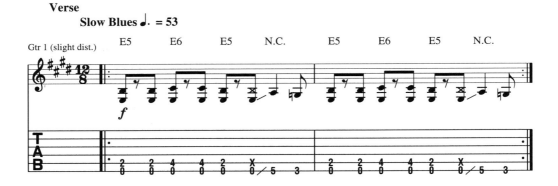

| **Artist:** Led Zeppelin | **Trivia:** Co-writer Willie Dixon was properly credited for |
|---|---|
| **Album:** *Led Zeppelin* | this song, along with "I Can't Quit You Baby," on Zeppelin's |
| **Year:** 1969 | debut album, but he filed a lawsuit and was awarded |
| **Guitarist:** Jimmy Page | damages for their use of portions of his songs "You Need Love" and "Bring It on Home" on *Led Zeppelin II*. |